CUBA

in pictures

972. 91

A modern lighthouse has been erected on the walls of Havana's historic Morro Castle.

**By NATHAN A. HAVERSTOCK
and JOHN P. HOOVER,**
THE LATIN AMERICAN SERVICE

STERLING PUBLISHING CO., INC.   **NEW YORK**

Oak Tree Press Co., Ltd. London & Sydney

VISUAL GEOGRAPHY SERIES

Afghanistan
Alaska
Argentina
Australia
Austria
Belgium and Luxembourg
Berlin—East and West
Bolivia
Brazil
Bulgaria

Canada
The Caribbean (English-
   Speaking Islands)
Ceylon (Sri Lanka)
Chile
China
Colombia
Costa Rica
Cuba
Czechoslovakia

Denmark
Ecuador ✓
Egypt
El Salvador
England
Ethiopia
Fiji
Finland
France
French Canada
Ghana
Greece
Greenland
Guatemala
Haiti
Hawaii
Holland
Honduras
Hong Kong
Hungary
Iceland
India
Indonesia
Iran
Iraq
Ireland
Islands of the
   Mediterranean
Israel
Italy
Jamaica
Japan
Kenya
Korea
Kuwait
Lebanon
Liberia
Malawi

Malaysia and Singapore
Mexico
Morocco
Nepal
New Zealand
Nicaragua
Norway
Pakistan and Bangladesh
Panama and the Canal
   Zone
Peru
The Philippines
Poland
Portugal
Puerto Rico
Rhodesia
Rumania
Russia
Saudi Arabia
Scotland
Senegal
South Africa
Spain
Surinam
Sweden
Switzerland
Tahiti and the
   French Islands of
   the Pacific
Taiwan
Tanzania
Thailand
Tunisia
Turkey
Venezuela
Wales
West Germany
Yugoslavia

This old cigar maker does his work by hand.

PICTURE CREDITS

The publishers wish to thank the following for the photographs used in this book: Cuban Embassy, London; Eastfo[...] New York; El Nuevo Dia, San Juan, Puerto Rico; Frank McDonald; Organization of American States, Washington, D.(] Lyle Stuart; Tass from Sovfoto, New York; John Wallach.

A new housing development has sprung up at Playa Giron, scene of the "Bay of Pigs" invasion.

CONTENTS

The skyline of modern Havana seen from the sea is not unlike Miami, only about 100 miles away across the Straits of Florida.

INTRODUCTION

BEGINNING in 1959 with the overthrow of a corrupt government by an armed guerrilla band, led by Fidel Castro, son of a wealthy landowner, the Republic of Cuba has been the scene of an experiment unique in the annals of Latin America—a Revolution that has led to the creation of the Western Hemisphere's first Marxist society.

Opinions are divided on the changes that have taken place in Cuba, many of which frankly sacrifice the good of the people for the good of the State. Some believe that the Castro régime provides a "model," which, with modification might be wisely employed by poor nations around the globe, frustrated by their inability to meet rising popular demands for land,

schools, and jobs with limited—often insufficient—human and financial resources.

Others regard Cuba since Castro as a textbook lesson in tyranny.

The controversy over the pros and cons of the Castro régime has been marked with an emotionalism which has obscured the problems of the Cuban people. For nearly a decade and a half, there have been no formal communications between the peoples of Cuba and the United States, following the latter country's severance of all cultural and diplomatic ties with the Caribbean nation on January 3, 1961.

The unhappy result is that the people of the United States have only a dimming memory of the ever-flowering beauty of an island often

5

Fidel Castro, Cuba's "Maximum Leader," exchanges views with workers.

called the "Pearl of the Antilles," lying just 90 miles off their shores. The Cuban people themselves have been subjected to an intense and incessant indoctrination, through all the channels of information open to them, in the evils of United States "imperialism." This propaganda has gone unchallenged, in the complete absence on the island of a free press, or the possibility of open contacts with the American people.

Like proud children in a game of blind man's buff, the two nations have stumbled very near the precipice of nuclear war, have created mutual fears of one another that are of more than life size, drawn up out of the stuff of fantasy. Only in very recent times, with the relaxation of East-West tensions flowing from the U.S. President's historic journeys in 1972 to Peking and Moscow is there some hope for the future of improved U.S.-Cuban relations.

Along with it, there is a growing recognition that Cuba's problems neither began nor ended with Castro's triumph and the 1959 Cuban Revolution.

This part of the port of Havana, built with Soviet aid, is one of the most modern dock areas in Latin America.

The rolling landscape of Cuba is well represented by this scene near the Yumuri River.

I. THE LAND

CUBA IS the largest of the Antilles, or islands of the West Indies, and has about half of all the land area of the islands in the Caribbean sea. It is about the size of Pennsylvania or of England minus Yorkshire—some 44,000 square miles—though of a different shape, 785 miles long and from 25 to 120 miles wide. If one end of Cuba were placed in New York City, the other would reach west of Chicago, or, if one end were placed in London, the other would come very near to Madrid.

Cuba is only 90 miles from the Florida coast at the nearest point, and about the same distance from Mexico's Yucatan peninsula. The important trade routes leading in and out of the Gulf of Mexico and the Caribbean pass along Cuba's northern and southern coasts. Ships and planes going to and from such important cities as Houston, New Orleans and Miami must pass near Cuba, from where enemy ships and planes could attack them.

About half of the Cuban countryside is gently rolling, level enough for the operation of farm machinery. Broad grasslands are found in the central part, and mountains rise at both the eastern and western ends, with a small mountainous area near the south coast at the island's mid-point.

In the rugged Sierra Maestra Mountains of eastern Cuba, a work crew fells trees to make way for a road.

In western Cuba, a long, low range of hills is known as the Organos Mountains, their highest peak stretching up only 2,500 feet. The Organos present a strange appearance, with their odd-shaped humps, often seeming bewitched or unreal. They are full of limestone caves, in which swarms of bats hang from the ceilings and walls. In the past, bat droppings—*guano*—were collected and used for fertilizer.

VEGETATION

About one fourth of Cuba is covered with mountain forests, chiefly pine in the west, and a rich variety elsewhere, including stands of valuable hardwoods—ebony, cedar, and mahogany, all of which are prized by furniture makers. Among the 30 species of palms, the stately royal palm, found in groves throughout the island, is easily the most distinctive. These trees are tall and slender, and their silver-grey trunks are crowned with deep green fronds. The walls of many *bohios*, or peasant huts, are made from their bark, and their leaves are used for thatching roofs. The royal palms do not bear edible fruit, but they are much admired by all who appreciate graceful beauty and are a popular subject of island artists.

Groves of banana and plantain "trees," which are really giant herbs and not trees at all, are a familiar sight. Plantains are very similar to bananas, but the fruit is starchy, not sweet, and is used as a vegetable. The banana and plantain, however, are not native to Cuba, but were introduced by the Spaniards. Another common tree of foreign origin is the mango, which has run wild in the eastern forests.

One of the tallest trees is the ceiba, or silk-cotton tree, which may reach 150 feet. In the densest forests are enormous vines or lianas, like the jagüey, which can strangle the largest trees in its coils.

In addition to the banana and mango, tropical

MOUNTAINS

The Sierra Maestra Mountains—scene of several guerrilla uprisings in Cuba's history—rise to nearly 8,000 feet along the southern and southeastern coast of Oriente, Cuba's easternmost province. Rugged and wild, the Sierra Maestra Mountains have few roads. Their slopes are heavily forested with tropical trees—some areas are almost as dense as rain-forests. Long vines hang from huge trees and orchids of many kinds cling to the branches and trunks. Toward the summits of the Sierra Maestra, where the temperatures are cooler, the vegetation becomes less tropical and—though there is no frost line—sparser.

Compared to the Sierra Maestra, the Trinidad Mountains near the south-central coast are not impressive. They are limited to a small area, with only a few peaks rising about 3,500 feet. They, too, are forested, though the stands of trees are smaller in size and less varied. Like the eastern mountains, the Trinidad range has provided havens for guerrillas and escaped slaves in times past. Today, good roads cross the range, as does a railway linking the island's north and south coasts.

8

These young men are climbing coconut palms to gather the nuts. Note the machete flanking the leg of the man at left.

fruits include the avocado, orange, lemon, prickly pear, custard apple, pawpaw and coconut. Brilliant flowering trees and shrubs grow wild as well as in gardens and parks everywhere. Among these are magnolias, jasmine, gardenias, jacaranda, frangipani, and most brilliant and abundant of all, the showy red, purple or orange bougainvillea.

The Isle of Pines has a booming citrus fruit industry. These workers are carefully planting young orange trees.

RIVERS AND COASTAL WATERS

Apart from some coastal swamps—the largest is Zapata Swamp, west of Cienfuegos on the south coast—the lands of Cuba are well drained. Most streams are short and, except in the rainy season, too shallow for navigation.

Cuba has many excellent natural ports, perhaps 200 of them, most with narrow mouths leading into peaceful deepwater coves and bays. Two dozen are in use today as shipping points for sugar and other products. Havana is the chief port, while other important ones are Santiago, Cienfuegos, Cardenas, Matanzas, Nuevitas, and Antilla. At Guantanamo, in Oriente province, the United States maintains a naval base, considered to be of major strategic importance.

Off the coast, coral reefs and islands form sheltered bays and lagoons, a prime attraction for snorkelers and scuba divers. The Isle of Pines, largest of the offshore islands, has an area of more than 1,000 square miles, and a sizeable population, raising cattle and growing citrus and other crops.

Cuba's most up-to-date sugar port is Cienfuegos, part of which is seen here. That is not sand next to the track, but granulated sugar that has fallen from the railway cars.

The entrance to the port of Santiago de Cuba is so rural in appearance that one would not guess that the second largest city of Cuba lies beyond it.

CLIMATE

Cuba's agreeable climate ranges from subtropical to tropical. Most of the time people find lightweight clothing most comfortable—such as Cuba's typical *guayabera*, a loose-hanging Caribbean shirt. Winter temperatures average 71 degrees Fahrenheit and summer, 82 degrees. The temperature rarely drops below 40 degrees or rises higher than 100.

Trade winds, which blow steadily off the ocean from east to west across the island, keep temperatures cool and the atmosphere fresh. Except when the sugar mills are grinding cane, there is little pollution. In the autumn, hurricanes sometimes rake the island, mainly the western part, and destroy crops, occasionally with loss of human life.

About 50 inches of rain can be expected during the May-October wet season, precisely when it is most needed to help the sugar cane grow to as much as 20 feet high. But the rains do not always come at regular intervals during the year, nor are they distributed evenly throughout the island. This explains why, for example, dense tropical rain-forests exist in the eastern part of Cuba, and in the middle of the island there are some dry, cactus-studded lowlands.

NATURAL RESOURCES

The land that produces tobacco, cattle and the all-important sugar cane is easily Cuba's most important natural resource. The island is also fairly well endowed with minerals, including nickel and copper, both mined commercially, and large reserves of iron ore in Oriente province. There are also small quantities of petroleum, and pockets of manganese and chrome, both valuable in steel-making.

Ocean resources come mainly from the Gulf Stream, which flows west to east nearly the entire length of the north coast. The Gulf Stream is rich in such commercially valuable fish as red snapper and swordfish, and the Cuban government is making a determined effort to expand its fishing industry.

11

Cuba has greatly expanded its fishing fleet. Here freshly-gathered sponges are strung up to dry in the rigging of a fishing boat.

Crocodiles are native to Cuban waters, but these specimens are a few of nearly 12,000 bred in captivity on a crocodile farm in the district of Sienagui de Sapatoz.

WILDLIFE

Unlike its fish and other marine life, Cuba's land animals have been all but wiped out. At one time the island had deer, rabbits, peccaries, squirrels, and several varieties of small wildcats. Few of these remain.

As a meeting ground for birds from both the tropical and temperate zones, Cuba is rich in bird life. Several species known in the summer in the United States spend the winter in Cuba, most notably the hummingbird. Other birds found in Cuba include the mockingbird and many kinds of warblers. As in other Caribbean lands, the buzzard wheeling high overhead is a common sight in Cuba. Among ocean species, gulls and terns and man-of-war—or frigate—birds, are often seen. Wading birds include flamingos, pelicans, roseate spoonbills, herons, and various kinds of snipes.

Reptiles and amphibians, apart from frogs and lizards, are not numerous, and poisonous snakes are unknown. The most spectacular reptile is the crocodile.

CITIES

HAVANA

No city in Cuba rivals the capital, Havana, in population, industry, public buildings, fine houses, or in importance as a governmental hub. With a population of about 1,000,000, Havana has grown outwards in layers or rings. The heart is the old, colonial city on the shores of Havana Bay. Surrounding this is the 19th-century city of warehouses, shops, some government buildings and old town houses. Farther out, in Vedado and other western suburbs, Havana has a modern appearance, comparable to that of other major Western-hemisphere cities.

Flamingos wade contentedly in a pool at the Havana Zoo.

Havana has hotels, night clubs, concert halls, and theatres, including the "Chaplin," formerly the "Blanquita," which has the greatest seating capacity of any theatre in the world—6,500 seats. The city's numerous dance groups play bongo drums, maracas, guitars, piano, and other familiar instruments. Cuba has many radio stations and several powerful television

At the upper right, the Morro Castle overlooks the main approach to the port of Havana.

Floats, drill teams and marching bands parade in three columns down a Havana boulevard on May Day.

The new residential district of Havana East provides comfortable apartments for thousands of Cuban workers.

stations—most Havana homes have a television set and almost all of them a radio or two. Havana also has a sports stadium, a race track, courts for jai-alai (a fast game involving a hard rubber ball hurled at an incredible speed from a basket strapped to the player's hand, and bounced off a hard wall). There are also many cinemas, bowling alleys, and places to buy popcorn, hot dogs and hamburgers.

With suburbs that stretch east and west along the coast from Morro Castle, a colonial fort at the mouth of the port, Havana is one of the world's great cities. A string of lights along the Malecón—or broad seafront avenue—has been called Havana's "diamond necklace." The city of Marianao (really a large suburb of Havana, of which it is a continuation) is one of Cuba's largest and most populous urban areas.

OTHER CITIES

West of Havana, Pinar del Rio is a sleepy, tropical town, important historically, but now in decline. East of Havana are two ports, Matanzas on the north coast and Cienfuegos on the south, both of which have lost importance in the past half century. Cienfuegos flourished through the 19th and early 20th centuries, but declined when railways and highways made shipments through Havana easier than through old-time provincial seaports.

In the middle of the island north of Cienfuegos is the provincial capital of Santa Clara, which has benefitted during the last decade from the Castro government's emphasis on building up Cuba's provinces. The old port of Trinidad, on the south coast east of Cienfuegos, is a jewel of colonial architecture. The port from which Hernando Cortez set sail for his conquest of Mexico, Trinidad has an ancient history, reflected in the buildings that still stand—hopefully awaiting restoration. Another city with colonial remains is the inland city of Sancti Spiritus.

Camaguey, with a population approaching 200,000, is the most important city between Havana and Santiago. Camaguey, with an international airport, is a sugar and rail hub, a major distribution point, and the home of a growing number of industries.

The second city of Cuba, Santiago, has a population of about 250,000 and lies on the south coast near the eastern end of the island. Santiago's climate is much warmer than that of Havana, and the vegetation surrounding it is lusher. Like Havana, the port of Santiago has a

A chessboard posted in a square in Camaguey shows the up-to-the-minute positions of the chessmen in the famous Fischer-Spassky match of 1972.

colonial fort at its entrance. It is also a major hub of Cuban trade and commerce, with rail, highway, and air connections with Havana and other important Cuban cities. The people of Santiago have always felt themselves different from the people of Havana. They are a breed apart, almost a separate nationality. They do not rush around as energetically as people of the capital; their pace of life is much more leisurely. Even their language is different—they speak with a lilting sing-song accent and use words and expressions not usually heard in Havana.

This "holiday village" for vacationers is situated on the Zapata Peninsula not very far from Havana.

In historic Havana, long thronged with tourists and pleasure-seekers, Raul Castro addresses a mass meeting of soldiers and workers.

2. HISTORY

CHRISTOPHER COLUMBUS discovered Cuba on October 27, 1492 while on his first voyage to the New World. Two years later, the great admiral paid a second brief visit to the island, before discovering Jamaica.

Before his arrival, it is estimated that Cuba had a population of 100,000 Arawak Indians, who had migrated to the lush green island in the unrecorded past by island-hopping stages up the chain of the Antilles from South America. Two Arawak groups—the Ciboneys and the Tainos—lived in a state of idyllic tranquillity before their discovery by the outside world—in a state of peace that has seldom been matched anywhere.

The Arawaks were Neolithic in culture. With stone and flint implements, they engaged in primitive farming—the growing of maize,

sweet potatoes, squash, chili peppers and other crops. They enriched their diet with fish, turtles, iguanas, snakes and birds. And they knew how to make pottery, baskets and cotton cloth.

The Indians lived in semi-permanent villages of round huts, slept in hammocks and smoked or snuffed tobacco. They ventured out upon the green sea around them in canoes large enough for ocean voyaging. Somehow they chose and obeyed tribal or clan leaders by a system.

The Spaniards were first known to the Arawaks as the men who raided their villages for slaves. By the time that the Spaniards came to settle in Cuba, some 20 years after its discovery, the Arawaks were wary. Pitting their bows and arrows against powder and ball, they tried to prevent the Spaniards from building a settlement at Baracoa in 1511. The Arawak

A few simple stone implements like these are all that remain of Cuba's pre-Columbian culture.

leader, Hatuey, became Cuba's first hero and martyr. As he was about to be burned at the stake, he spurned an invitation to accept Christianity, noting that a Heaven populated by Christians held little attraction for him.

There followed a two-year conquest of the island, directed by Governor Diego Velasquez, a man schooled in cruelty and avarice by 18 years' experience in the nearby island of Hispaniola. After defeating the Indians, Velasquez put them to "useful" work, digging what gold there was out of the earth and sifting it out of the streams.

From that largely fruitless task, the hapless Arawaks were rounded up by force and resettled on *encomiendas*, or large ranches, to work the fields. But the Indians proved little suited to such serfdom, and soon the island's Spanish magistrates introduced Negro slavery. Beginning in 1515, about 1,000,000 blacks were eventually settled in Cuba.

Long before that occurred, Hernando Cortez set out from Cuba to the Mexican coast to conquer the Aztec empire. Despairing of making a quick fortune in Cuba, many Spaniards flocked to the banner of Cortez.

Unhappily, their departure did not save the Arawaks. By the middle of the 16th century, their numbers had been woefully reduced. No more than 5,000 remained alive, the rest had died off—victims of cruel treatment and European-introduced diseases. Their passing meant little to Spain, which was disappointed in the profits of Cuba, as compared with the great riches that flowed from the looted Aztec civilization of Mexico.

The Spanish crown did see fit to issue a royal order prohibiting future inhumane abuses of the Arawaks. But as was true in other colonies that yielded little profit in gold, the Spanish monarchs made little effort to enforce this order.

Cuba languished through more than three centuries under official neglect. To the people of Cuba, the far-off royal government seemed little more than an irksome burden—the dead weight of Spanish authority seemed destined to crush whatever stirrings of enterprise might have been expected to crop up even in a poor island colony.

17th-CENTURY HAVANA

Havana rose to prominence as a military stronghold during the 17th century. In its heavily fortified port, galleons homeward bound for Spain assembled to make the Atlantic crossing in the protection of a naval convoy. Over a period of months, galleons from near and far would anchor in the safe refuge of Havana—vessels laden with Indian gold and emeralds from Colombia, Inca treasure from Peru and Ecuador, glittering silver from the fabulous mines at Potosí in Bolivia, and precious metals in abundance from the wealthy empire of the Aztecs in Mexico. There were also galleons whose precious cargoes had originated across the far Pacific in the Orient and been transhipped

19

across Mexico, and loaded again on ships bound for Havana and the Old World.

Year after year, after the hurricane season had passed, a great fleet would gather at Havana. High-pooped ships rode heavy in the water from the weight of gold and silver bullion, colonial raw materials—sugar, hides, cotton, and dyewoods. Black-gowned priests, portly officials, and prosperous settlers and their families returning to Spain made endless preparations to carry back whatever of value had been wrung out the colonies. On those treasure fleets depended not only the survival of the Spanish empire, but also the economies of many of the European nations.

In the shadow of the moss-covered and forbidding walls of Havana's forts, the crews of the fleet and their passengers—together with tradesmen, slaves, soldiers, and others—would fill the days, weeks and months of waiting for uncertain sailing dates with rowdy amusements. The transients were gouged by the local population, and many even sickened and died from the recurrent pestilences that broke out in the city.

Confused lines of authority within the Spanish empire thwarted all efforts to control the situation, and Havana's historical tradition and character were established in the days of the treasure fleets. The city was thereafter known for crime, gambling, and prostitution—vice which were to endure until the Castro era.

Added to these were two other unlawful pursuits, smuggling and pirate raids. Cuba has far too many good places for a ship to anchor for effective patrol or surveillance. Cubans of the colonial period had ample opportunity for illicit trade with pirates, with foreign powers, with anyone who would take their hides, meat, and timber and exchange them for finished goods or slaves.

Cuban history is full of stories of pirate raids. In 1603, for example, a naval outlaw flying the pirate flag sacked and burned Santiago de Cuba, the nation's second city even then located some 700 miles from the protection of Havana's guns. Two decades later, a Dutch pirate captured an entire Spanish treasure fleet off Cuba's north coast—a severe blow to the treasure-dependent economy of Spain.

The raiders hailed from several nations. In 1662, British settlers from Jamaica burned and pillaged Santiago once again. Three years later, the British and their French allies took Sancti Spiritus, another Cuban town of some consequence. Corsairs from the pirate den on

The British flag flies over Havana and flutters from the sterns of British ships at anchor during 1762, when Cuba was ruled by London rather than Madrid.

Tortuga island, off Haiti's north coast, swarmed at will over Cuba, as did raiders from bases closer at hand, the Isle of Pines and other off-coast islands near Cuba. The legendary Englishman, Henry Morgan, repeatedly pillaged Cuban settlements for 30 years, from 1668 until the end of the century.

Harassed and discouraged, the settlers of Cuba were slow to add to their numbers. During the entire 17th century, the population of the Cuban colony increased from only 30,000 to 60,000. There was little new industry—some shipbuilding in Havana, a copper mine near Santiago, and the first sugar cane and tobacco plantations. By the end of the century, it is estimated that there were 100 small mills in operation, grinding sugar cane with either human or animal power—forerunners of an industry that would dominate Cuba and Cubans in the centuries to follow.

18th-CENTURY PROSPERITY

The fortunes of Cuba improved during the 18th century. One reason was that a new and relatively progressive royal family, the Bourbons, took over the Spanish Crown from the decaying Hapsburgs in 1700. The French-influenced Bourbon monarchs carried out needed reforms in both Spain and Cuba. Havana's economy benefitted from the presence of the French fleet, which used the city as a base for launching assaults on British territories in the Caribbean—an extension of Old World feuds.

Unlike their predecessors, Bourbon administrators in Cuba were likely to be competent and efficient, if on occasions harsh as well. The Bourbons set up a new system whereby the island's profitable tobacco trade was put in the hands of a government-run monopoly. Small-

21

The city of Havana was a sleepy provincial town in 1800, as this sketch of the city's market-place shows

scale Cuban tobacco growers, hurt by the move, took the lead in a revolt in 1717 that was put down only after much blood had been shed.

A similar monopoly was established to handle all of the island colony's import and export trade, much to the displeasure of Cubans, who concluded correctly that one purpose of the monopoly was to restrict trade and keep local prices for imports high. The consumers of colonial Cuba were thus given an object lesson in how imperialism works.

But to their credit, the Bourbons also brought a beginning of intellectual and cultural life to Cuba, including the establishment of a seminary and a secondary school early in the century and the installation of the first printing press in 1720. The founding of the University of Havana added to the colony's prestige, and the construction of the Cathedral of Havana and other public buildings symbolized the coming of age of the Cuban colony.

War between Spain and England at mid-century turned the Caribbean into a danger zone. The British occupied Guantanamo and threatened both Santiago and Havana in 1740. Later on, in 1762, the British occupied Havana and held it for more than a year.

Though British rule was of short duration, many reforms and progressive changes were introduced. Commercial activity boomed— slaves and European merchandise poured into the port of Havana and exports increased sharply. The eyes of the Cubans were opened to the blessings of commerce free of the repressive monopolies of Spain.

By 1774, the colony had 171,000 people— 96,000 whites, 44,000 black slaves, and 31,000 persons of mixed blood. The economy was surging ahead, tobacco production greatly increased, the number of sugar mills quintupled, and Cuba's trade for the first time began to contribute importantly to the wealth of Spain. A further boost to Cuba's economy came when Spain allowed the colony to trade with the young United States after 1779—Spain having helped the rebellious Thirteen Colonies in their

In 1857, black slaves were still at work in sugar mills—slavery was not completely abolished in Cuba until 1886.

struggle for independence (as a way of getting back at the British).

Reflecting the new prosperity, public and private construction in Havana gave the city a new and definite character—the enduring charm of its colonial architecture. New ideas began to take root in the city, too, some of them borrowed from the French Revolution.

At the same time, political turmoil elsewhere in the Caribbean worked to Cuba's benefit. A revolt against France in nearby Haiti led to the destruction of the Haitian sugar industry, and the influx into Cuba of some 30,000 French refugees, who brought with them improved sugar-industry technology. Then, in 1795, Spain ceded Santo Domingo, the Spanish-owned part of the island of Hispaniola, to France. This led to the transfer of the ruling Spanish *audiencia*, the administrative seat of government, together with the Catholic archbishopric, from Santo Domingo to Cuba. In 1801, Haiti invaded Santo Domingo and thousands of Spaniards fled to Cuba, and numerous other Frenchmen and

Spaniards moved to Cuba from New Orleans after France sold the vast Louisiana territory to the United States in 1803.

THE LAST CENTURY OF SPANISH RULE

During the wars for independence elsewhere in Latin America in the early 19th century, Cuba remained comparatively quiet. The island's Spanish officials easily survived a few minor plots. A few people advocated joining the United States, but this notion had very little support at that time.

Liberal ideas, sparked by Simón Bolívar's remarkable success in liberating Venezuela, Colombia, Ecuador, Peru and Bolivia, began to trickle into Cuba. Cuban dissatisfaction grew sharply, however, under the crude and tyrannical rule of Spain's Ferdinand VII. Popular dislike of this king was strengthened by the widening breach between the Cuban-born "creoles" and the Spanish-born "peninsulares." The latter dominated local government and

23

Medical students of the 1870's prepare to face the firing squad, after taking part in independence activities.

business. A few creole radicals and independence advocates, fed up with a system that reserved to Spain and the Spanish-born the profits of Cuban toil, had to flee to escape harsh repressive measures, including an 1825 decree that empowered the captain-general to suspend laws and to exile anyone he chose.

However, during the first half of the 19th century, most Cubans were too caught up in the island's rapid economic growth to have much time for rebellion. Sugar production had by now become the dominant industry. Technological advances, the use of steam-driven grinding machinery, for example, were laying the base for a further expansion of this profitable activity. By 1827, the island recorded a population of 704,000—and 1,000 sugar mills, 30,000 ranches, 5,500 tobacco farms, and 2,100 coffee plantations.

As the national wealth grew, however, the friction between Cuban creoles and Spanish administrators grew also. Not surprisingly, the United States had replaced Spain as Cuba's most important trading partner by the 1840's. This commercial interest led to some agitation for annexation to the United States, backed by the appeal of the United States to the slave-holding elements in Cuba as a country in which the slave-owning class was still powerful.

Between 1848 and 1851, there were three revolutionary expeditions to Cuba led by Narciso

Lopéz, a Venezuelan royalist-turned-rebel who had some unofficial support and backing from groups in the United States. All three invasions were defeated, but by 1868 a native independence insurrection had taken hold in mountainous eastern Cuba, which was to last for a decade.

During this Ten Years' War the island was racked by civil conflict, with rebels receiving secret aid and comfort from elements in the United States. Officially, Presidents Grant and Hayes limited themselves to urging the warring parties to reach a settlement of their differences. But before the war had worn itself out, both sides had lost heavily, and much of Cuba, especially the eastern area of the island, was in ruins.

In accordance with peace terms reached in 1878, a general amnesty was granted all involved in the revolt. Slaves who had fought for either side were freed. Cuba was to be converted from a colony to an integral administrative unit of Spain. But this change was scarcely enough to stop popular demands for independence.

For the rebellion had brought important economic changes. Coffee cultivation had been virtually abandoned. Much of the island's cigar-making industry had migrated to nearby Florida. Only the sugar industry boomed, and that largely as the result of U.S. investment and tariff preferences. The suspension of this ad-

24

The Cuban Revolutionary Committee meeting in New York in 1892 prepared for Cuba's fight for independence from Spain.

vantage in 1894 was among the chief factors leading to a renewal of Cuban rebellion in 1895.

JOSÉ MARTÍ

The chief promoter, propagandist, and organizer of the insurrection that led to Independence was José Martí, who had been involved in the Ten Years' War and deported

for subversion. By 1892, already recognized as the "Apostle" of a free Cuba, Martí mobilized Cuban exiles in the U.S. and organized a revolutionary junta—or, committee—in New York City. He also took the lead in making contacts with potential allies in Cuba and elsewhere, raised funds, and, after some jousting with U.S. authorities, landed with an armed force in eastern Cuba in February, 1895. Martí was killed in a skirmish with loyalist troops on the plains of Dos Rios, in Oriente province, and thus became Free Cuba's martyr.

THE "REPUBLIC IN ARMS"

By September, the rebels had proclaimed a "Republic in Arms." Fighting soon spread to all parts of the island and became increasingly bitter. Using the hit-and-run tactics of the guerrilla, rebel forces were usually able to evade frontal encounters with regular Spanish troops, and occasionally even to defeat them in conventional battles.

The island was reduced to anarchy. Sympathy for the rebels and their cause grew in the United States. Pressed repeatedly to intervene in Cuba—at least to grant belligerent rights to

José Martí, the "Apostle of a Free Cuba," was photographed in a moment of repose shortly before his death in battle in 1895.

During the 1898 War of Independence, Cuban farmers like these flocked to the side of the rebels and were hastily organized as militiamen.

the rebels—both Presidents Cleveland and McKinley refused. But stories of atrocities perpetrated by the Spaniards, fanned by the so-called "yellow press" in the United States, became more numerous. President McKinley finally warned Spain to ease up in its brutal repression. Secretly, the President undertook efforts to persuade Spain to sell Cuba to the U.S.

In Cuba, the war dragged on and all efforts at conciliation seemed futile. Severe rioting in Havana in January, 1898, led the American consul there to request a warship to protect the lives of American citizens. The battleship *Maine* was sent to the scene, but within days of its arrival in Havana, it was blown up and sunk with the loss of many American lives.

Popular resentment over the sinking of the *Maine* forced President McKinley to demand that Spain give in to Cuban demands for free-

dom without delay. When Spain refused McKinley asked Congress for authorization to use force to put an end to Spanish rule in Cuba Congressional authorization was granted, with an official disclaimer of any intention to annex Cuba, on April 25, 1898, and the Spanish American War began.

THE SPANISH-AMERICAN WAR

The ensuing conflict lasted only four months Cuban insurgents already had effective contro over most of the island, except for scattere strong-points still in the hands of a relativel large Spanish army. The plan of the U.S. arme forces was to defeat the Spanish navy bottle up in the port of Santiago de Cuba, and t convince the Spanish army that its defeat wa inevitable.

The death of a rebel during the 1898 War of Independence is a popular subject for Cuban artists and illustrators.

The latter objective was achieved first, on July 1, when the U.S. forces, after bloody assaults, took San Juan Hill and El Caney, near Santiago de Cuba, actions that made Colonel Theodore Roosevelt and his "Rough Riders" heroes in the eyes of the American public overnight. Two days later the Spanish fleet steamed out of Santiago and into the gun-sights of the waiting U.S. Navy, which sent the poorly commanded fleet to the bottom.

Elsewhere in the far-flung Spanish-American War, the U.S. scored quick victories. Spanish naval forces in the Philippines were destroyed and Puerto Rico was occupied with only slight resistance. On August 2, Spain agreed to relinquish sovereignty over Cuba and hostilities came to an end.

UNITED STATES RULE

Modern Cuban history thus began under the U.S., not the Cuban, flag. Unfortunately, a series of misunderstandings soured relations between the U.S. forces and Cuban rebels almost from the first. These were compounded

Rebel troops in action during the 1898 War of Independence.

27

The "Surrender Tree" is near the spot where Colonel Theodore Roosevelt and his Rough Riders won the battle of San Juan Hill.

by the "culture shock" of U.S. troops on seeing at close range a society which they were prepared neither by language nor experience to understand.

Owing to these ill feelings, the Cubans were even denied participation in ceremonies transferring sovereignty from Spain to the United States on January 1, 1898! From then until 1902, the U.S. military government maintained order, built schools, improved sanitation, tightened up revenue collections, and organized a local constabulary. In all, the U.S. military authorities did all of those things that would in their eyes make occupied Cuba conform to the American rather than the Cuban scale of cultural, social and political values. The result was that Cuba became a client state—a protectorate—of the United States.

INDEPENDENCE

That this was clearly the intention of the United States is confirmed by subsequent documents relating to Cuban "independence." In early 1901, for example, a Cuban Constitution was drafted under U.S. supervision. The Cubans were forced to include in this document

the provisions of the so-called Platt Amendment, which forbade their new nation from contracting any foreign indebtedness which it could not pay out of ordinary revenues. It further forbade any treaty that would impair Cuba's sovereignty, and provided for the establishment of two U.S. naval stations on Cuban territory.

Lest there be any doubt that the U.S. was the guarantor of Cuban independence, the Amendment further provided that Cuba should acknowledge the validity of all acts of the U.S. military authorities during the occupation, leave in abeyance the future sovereignty of the Isle of Pines, and accept the right of the United States to intervene in Cuban affairs—whenever it was felt necessary to protect Cuba's independence or to maintain a Cuban government able to protect life, liberty and property.

These conditions were imposed over the protests of most Cuban leaders. Opposition to them was also forthcoming from some circles in the United States. The basis of future relations between Cuba and its patron, the United States, was further spelled out in a treaty of 1903. This included economic inducements, a 20 per cent reduction on import duties for Cuban products

During the 1920's, sugar prices soared and many Cubans spent the profits in carefree and extravagant living—as in this Carnival scene on the Havana waterfront.

shipped to the U.S. market, and tariff preferences for U.S. goods exported to Cuba.

Cuban self-government formally began on May 20, 1902. From that date, the new nation was troubled by economic problems and the continuing after-effects of the destructive rebellion. From the quarrels among Cuban leaders, two political parties emerged—the Moderates and the Liberals. In late 1905, Tomás Estrada Palma, Cuba's first President under its new Constitution, was re-elected, only after opposition candidates withdrew from the race. Revolts sputtered on the island and the U.S. intervened and stayed until 1909.

There followed a succession of undistinguished Cuban rulers, whose régimes were mainly noteworthy for the corruption and popular agitation. The 1920's brought a new high in

sugar prices and prosperity to Cuba, which tided the island republic over, even into the early years of the U.S. depression of the 1930's. But as the economic bubble burst in Cuba, the nation's ruler, President Gerardo Machado, was forced to use increasingly harsh methods for controlling revolutionary discontent. Eventually, Machado himself was forced to flee Cuba, to seek asylum in the nearby Bahamas in August, 1933.

FULGENCIO BATISTA

Machado's departure was the signal for anarchy. The reins of government were seized on September 4, 1933 by a Cuban army sergeant, Fulgencio Batista. Batista immediately took command of the nation's armed forces, and thereby became undisputed master of Cuba—

29

Gambling was wide open in pre-Castro Cuba, when Havana's Gran Casino Nacional swarmed with pleasure-seekers.

with the approval, historians note, of a Cuban people anxious for an end to economic drift.

Despite requests from its own ambassador at Havana, the United States—respectful of its newly enunciated "Good Neighbor" policy—refused to intervene. Batista was not again challenged, and with interruptions he controlled Cuba for the next 25 years.

Up until 1940, Batista exercised his control by being commander-in-chief of the armed forces. He served as president from 1940 to 1944, proving to be a strong chief of state, but not a dictator. While he brooked no upset of the political and economic order, the customary democratic freedoms of press, assembly, speech and religion were not seriously restricted.

A clever man, Batista maintained his appeal to the mass of the Cuban people, while being careful to placate Cuba's propertied classes and to keep in the good graces of the United States. One of his earliest achievements, and one that won him great popularity among the Cuban people, was to win from the United States, in 1934, the cancellation of the Platt Amendment —the hated symbol of Cuba's humiliating status as a protectorate.

As President during World War II, Batista became a close collaborator of the United States and outspoken champion of the Allied cause,

stands from which both Cuba and Batista profited. In 1944, Batista ran for re-election, but was defeated by Ramón Grau San Martín, a

The pool of the Hotel Presidente in Havana as it appeared in 1955 recalls the days when tourism was a major industry in Cuba and Havana was a mecca for tourists from the United States.

This float at the 1972 Carnival commemorates Castro's attack on the Moncada Barracks.

widely admired university professor. Though an idealist, the professor actually headed a government that was only superficially free from the corruption that had lost Batista the presidency.

The administration of Grau's hand-picked successor, Carlos Prio Socarras, saw little improvement in the morality of public life and a lessening of the government's effectiveness. Batista, waiting in the wings, staged his second successful coup d'état in March, 1952. The pretext for his take-over was Prio's alleged plan to call off elections scheduled for 1952.

Batista lost little time in assembling an effective administration in terms of order, material welfare, and corruption limited to a chosen few.

On the surface, the times in Cuba were prosperous. U.S. tourists swarmed all over the island, gambling and vice flourished, and money flowed—some of it to line the pockets of corrupt politicians. But outside the glossy new suburbs of affluent Havana, there were Cubans in city ghettoes and in the vast expanse of the countryside who were far from happy with their lot.

THE CASTRO INSURRECTION

They cheered on July 26, 1953, when a band of young men, led by Fidel Castro, attacked the Moncada Barracks, an army garrison in Santiago de Cuba, and uprisings occurred simultaneously elsewhere on the island. But the attempted revolt failed, and Castro himself was consigned, after a trial, to a prison, from which he did not emerge until reprieved by a general amnesty declared by Batista in May, 1955.

After a brief sojourn in Havana, Castro, whose idealism had endeared him to large numbers of the Cuban people, went to Mexico, to plot Batista's downfall once more. In December, 1956, the youthful rebel with a small but determined band of 81 followers, landed in Oriente province, intending to carry on a guerilla campaign against the Batista government. All but a handful of the rebels were killed or captured by government troops—only about a dozen, including Castro, made it to mountain hideaways.

During the course of succeeding months,

recruits, supplies and public support flowed to Castro and his rebel band. The daring raids and forays carried out by the guerillas won them increased public sympathy within Cuba, and attracted growing aid in money and arms from secret sources in the United States.

Castro made skilful use of both radio and newspaper media in attracting world-wide support for his "26th of July Movement"— named after the date of his earlier, unsuccessful raid on the Moncada Barracks. Correspondents in the United States portrayed his struggle in a sympathetic light, and emphasized in grim detail the bloody reprisals carried out by the Batista government.

Student agitation in Cuba grew so violent that universities and even high schools had to be closed down. In April, 1958, Castro's call for a general strike, while failing to bring the Cuban economy to a halt, succeeded to the extent that the U.S. government cancelled all permits to ship arms to Batista. Amid such woes, Batista seemed scarcely to appreciate the danger, and procceeded with plans for 1958 elections, as though nothing was wrong.

In Washington, meanwhile, a distinct change of heart was taking place. Neither President Eisenhower nor his Secretary of State, nor even their ambassador in Havana felt that the U.S. should support Batista any longer, a man whose brutal put-down of courageous rebels was making him unpopular in the eyes of the world. U.S. officials let it be known that they would endure Batista only as long as elections scheduled for November, 1958, were open and honest.

But the elections proved to be a farce. Though Batista's hand-picked candidate won, the majority of the Cuban people boycotted the balloting. Batista thereupon ordered his army to make an overwhelming effort to destroy the rebels. But the result was a shock—his well equipped forces refused to fight, when confronted by an "enemy" with whom substantial numbers of his troops sympathized. Batista's army melted away.

In Havana, Batista, after a sober stock-taking on New Year's Eve, decided that further resistance was futile. In the early hours of the morning of January 1, 1959, he flew to sudden self-imposed exile, followed later in the day by thousands of his partisans. The people of Havana crowded out into the streets of the festive old capital to hail Batista's successor. Batista's first place of refuge was the Dominican Republic, but later settled in Madeira, and then Lisbon before his death in Spain in 1973.

THE CUBAN REVOLUTION

The success of what has come to be known as "The Cuban Revolution" has brought Cuba to the forefront of world attention, and the world itself to the threshold of nuclear war. For the Cuban people, it has meant a complete

change in the political system under which they live, the organization of the nation's economy, the ideas taught their children at schools—in all, change in every aspect of Cuban society.

At first many people outside Cuba, as well as within, were pleased by Castro's victory. The fact that the bearded guerrilla leader, against almost impossible odds, had succeeded in overthrowing a corrupt and well armed government, stirred widespread admiration. But others, who chose to reserve judgment on the change in Cuba until Castro had more clearly outlined his plans for the future, were skeptical. Their numbers grew as the new régime executed hundreds of opposition Cubans before firing squads, after "trials" scarcely worthy of the name. The number of critics multiplied even faster, with defections even among some of those who had fought alongside Castro in the rebellion, once it became clear that their leader was determined to make Cuba the Western hemisphere's first full-fledged socialist nation.

In working toward this undeclared goal, the Castro government, by the end of 1960 had taken over most foreign-owned and much Cuban-owned property, part of a swift transition from a private-enterprise to a state-controlled system. U.S. citizens were major losers in the takeovers, their losses in sugar mills, banks, hotels, utility companies, mines and farms—even apartment houses, personal residences and vacation homes—calculated at about U.S. $2,000,000,000.

In retaliation for these losses, the U.S. government stopped buying Cuban sugar, mainstay of the island's economy. This was a serious blow to Cuba, because sugar sales to the United States had been worth more than U.S. $500,000,000 a year. Equally serious to the Cuban economy, as relations between the U.S. and Cuba worsened, was the loss of further U.S. private investments and the virtual stopping of the visits to Cuba of U.S. tourists, whose spending had constituted another major source of Cuban earnings.

DIPLOMATIC RELATIONS ENDED

In January, 1961, just two years after Castro had taken power, the U.S. formally broke off all diplomatic relations with Cuba, which meant that the two governments no longer communicated with each other. By this time, there was little for the two governments to discuss. Trade and commerce had come to a halt, and it became clear that Castro was creating a whole new social order and economic structure—that he was changing Cuba from a democracy to a dictatorship copied after the Soviet Union and, to some extent, the People's Republic of China. Under this new system, the interests of individual Cubans were to be less important than what Castro declared to be the interests of the Revolution.

Castro himself relished his role as *lider maximo* (maximum leader) of the Revolution. He allowed Cuban embassies throughout Latin America to become headquarters for revolutionary propaganda. His goal, he declared, was to

33

see Cuba become the leader in starting what he calls "wars of liberation" throughout Latin America.

THE BAY OF PIGS INVASION

As might be expected, other Latin American nations were not happy with his dream, nor was the United States. In 1961, a group of Cuban exiles—backed, trained and armed secretly by the United States—invaded Cuba in the hope that the Cuban people would join them and rise up to topple Castro from power.

What did happen was quite different: the invading force was quickly defeated and taken prisoner. The whole fiasco is known as "The Bay of Pigs" from the name of the bay where the invaders landed, and to Cubans as "Playa Giron" after the beach on which the battle was fought. "Bay of Pigs" has since become, in the United States, a way of saying "disgraceful military defeat." Cubans, by contrast, hail "Playa Giron" as the first major defeat of U.S. imperialism in the Western hemisphere.

Eight months after the Bay of Pigs, Castro declared, "I am a Marxist-Leninist and will be a Marxist-Leninist until the last day of my life." From that moment, Cuba became officially allied with the Communist countries of the world.

There is considerable controversy over just when Castro decided to cast his lot with Communism. Some critics say that the United States drove him to make his declaration, by cutting off all trade with Cuba. Others take the position that Castro's devotion to Communism really began long ago, in his student days.

A month after his declaration, the Organization of American States, an association of the nations of the western hemisphere—with strong U.S. support, excluded Cuba from active membership on grounds that its Communist orientation made it impossible for Cuba to participate in an organization dedicated to the principles of representative democracy. In part, this decision was motivated by mounting fears that, under Castro, Cuba was becoming overly active in its support of rebellion elsewhere in the hemisphere.

MISSILE CRISIS

The situation became dramatically worse in the summer of 1962, when it became known that Cuba was receiving large quantities of military equipment from Russia, and that Soviet technicians were arriving in Cuba in large numbers. In October, President John F. Kennedy told a startled American public over nationwide television that the Russians had installed on Cuban soil missile bases capable of launching nuclear attacks on major cities of the United States and of Latin American countries.

The President demanded that the missiles be removed and threatened to use force to see that they were. A few days later the Russians agreed to remove the missiles and a nuclear war was avoided.

These Cuban documents outlining plans for revolutionary actions in Argentina were removed from the Cuban embassy in Buenos Aires by a defecting diplomat.

For Castro himself, the Russian decision was something of a set-back. He personally wanted to keep the missile sites intact, no matter what the consequences, on grounds that the Cuban government alone should decide the uses to which its territory should be put. In knuckling under to the Russians, Castro suffered a loss of prestige in the eyes of his fellow revolutionaries at home and abroad.

For its part, the United States agreed not to support another invasion of Cuba, and has remained faithful to this pledge, even clamping down on the use of U.S. territory by Cuban exile groups. But while keeping its word on the military side, the U.S. took severe economic measures against Cuba. For example, in 1964 it supported a move whereby all members of the Organization of American States except Mexico voted collectively to break off all trade and diplomatic relations with Cuba. This O.A.S. action was prompted by a formal complaint by Venezuela, which charged that the Castro government was providing arms to guerillas active in Venezuela.

While such actions have not brought about the downfall of the Castro government, they have meant that for many years there has been virtually no economic, social, or cultural inter-change between Cuba and other Western hemisphere nations. What contacts have remained have been underground, or secret ones, presumably related to guerrilla and other revolutionary activities.

During this period, U.S.-Cuban relations have been marked by distrust and hostility, with both nations dependent for information about the other on monitored radio broadcasts, stories written by correspondents from other nations, and secret intelligence reports. U.S. government officials insist that there are two main obstacles to improved relations with Cuba: the continuing presence of Soviet military forces on the island, and Cuba's continuing support for revolution elsewhere in the hemisphere.

These issues have been inflamed by others, most notably the hijacking of U.S. commercial airliners to Cuba, with Cuba refusing to return the perpetrators of the crime. In 1973, there was a first hopeful step on the way to improved relations, when the two countries, through Czech and Swiss diplomatic channels, worked out an agreement providing for prompt, certain, and severe punishment by Cuba for hijackers.

Further hope was seen in President Richard Nixon's 1972 visits to Moscow and Peking, journeys aimed at relaxing world tensions and

In 1960, the Russian deputy premier, Anastas Mikoyan (right) visited Castro in Cuba. In the middle is the legendary Che Guevara.

in creating a climate for what the President called "A Generation of Peace." In recent years, Cuba has also seemed to reduce its support for armed revolutions. Experts date this trend to the 1967 killing of Ernesto Che Guevara, who had been a trusted lieutenant of Castro's during the Cuban rebellion. Guevara had gone to Bolivia in the hope of fomenting a "Vietnam"-type situation there.

Castro himself, buoyed by the 1970 election victory of Salvador Allende, a Marxist candidate for the Presidency in Chile, hoped for a while that other American nations might enter upon the road to socialism via democratic processes. But his support of Allende could not prevent the overthrow of Marxism in Chile after that nation failed to solve its economic problems.

The problems to be resolved in improving U.S.-Cuban relations are many and complex. In working toward their resolution, Cuba could become a testing ground where new formulas for living together between differently organized societies could be worked out. This is the hope of those who point out that for four centuries Cuba was a colony of Spain; during most of this century dominated by its nearness to the United States; and in recent years dependent on the Soviet Union for such vital supplies as oil and machinery for its economy. Now, will Cuba finally emerge as something of a go-between in East-West affairs?

Even if this positive future rôle should fall to Cuba, there remains the island's need to depend on some big foreign power. That is the way it has always been with Cuba—first dependency on Spain, then the United States, and now on the Soviet Union.

To change this situation would appear beyond the power of any Cuban government. For the basic truth is that Cuba must import most of the things it needs and, to pay for them, has only its sugar to export. Only a big power can guarantee the market Cuba must have for its sugar.

Fidel Castro addresses a May Day rally. The sign on the building says in Spanish "Long live the socialist revolution and the first of May."

3. GOVERNMENT

THE REPUBLIC of Cuba has had no elections since Castro came to power. There is a president (appointed by Castro) who has no real power. The legislature is a 23-man Council of Ministers, all appointed by Castro, who is prime minister and first secretary of the Cuban Communist Party. In theory the council exercises both executive and legislative powers, but in practice Castro himself makes virtually all decisions.

Cuba is actually ruled by decree and has been so since 1959 when the Constitution of 1940 was suspended and replaced by the Fundamental Law of the Republic, authorizing the present set-up. To enforce the decrees of the Council, the Cuban government employs the largest internal security force in Latin America.

Opinions continue to be sharply divided on the profound changes that have taken place in Cuba under the Castro régime. Some believe that Castro has introduced needed and long overdue social reforms—that can only be provided by governments truly dedicated to the welfare of the masses and managed through some socialist scheme that puts the government in effective control of all of the problems and profits of production.

Poor nations, like Cuba, they say, can no longer afford the luxury of capitalism. They go on to say that the two thirds of the world's people who live in underdeveloped and foreign-dominated societies, must wage "wars of liberation" to achieve their economic independence, and use Cuba as a textbook model.

Others regard Cuba since Castro as an object

Some of the nearly 500,000 Cuban exiles in the United States as they arrived at Key West, Florida, in January, 1963.

lesson in tyranny. Critics of the Castro government, while conceding its sense of dedication and its obvious accomplishments in providing better health, housing and educational opportunities for the masses of the Cuban people, say that the price of such reforms has been too high. Social progress has been bought at an incalculable loss in personal freedom—including thousands of political prisoners—disruptions and shortages in the nation's economy, and the alienation of some 450,000 Cubans who have sought refuge in the United States.

POLICY TOWARDS THE UNITED STATES

In recent years, American intelligence experts have noted a lessening of Russian military activity in Cuba. What missiles remain are defensive in nature, they say, and pose no threat to the U.S. Some authorities, however, argue that the Russian presence in Cuba still constitutes a security threat, because the island provides the Soviets with naval facilities for nuclear-armed submarines—a base for expan-

"Alerta," the watchword of Cuba's armed forces, is featured in a poster showing soldiers with equipment provided by the Communist bloc.

38

About 200 Cubans still work on the United States Naval Base at Guantanamo. During World War II, 7,000 Cubans commuted to work on the base in a different atmosphere than the one prevailing today. Here workers are leaving Guantanamo at the end of the day, to re-enter Castro's Cuba.

Women carrying the Cuban flag on May Day, the international socialist day of celebration.

sion of Soviet influence in the Caribbean, long considered an American lake.

But there seems little arguing that it would be to the advantage of the superpowers to see a relaxation of the tension between Cuba and the United States. The restoration of diplomatic relations between the two countries, say officials advocating such a move, would help minimize whatever security threat is posed by continued Russian military presence on the island.

Publicly, however, Castro himself has given only slight indication that he would welcome an improvement of relations with the U.S. Before progress could be made toward this goal, a number of thorny problems would have to be resolved. For example, Castro has repeatedly stressed that the U.S. must evacuate the naval base at Guantanamo. Secondly, there is the influence of the large community of Cuban exiles in the United States, some of whom are influential in promoting their wish to see the Cuban leader toppled from power.

Another obstacle to more normal relation-

ships is the matter of compensation of U.S. citizens, whose properties were taken over by the Castro government.

Assuming steps are taken to improve relations with Cuba, the re-allocation of U.S. sugar quotas poses another hurdle to be overcome.

Raul Castro (left), brother of Fidel, holds the title of Vice Prime Minister in the Cuban government. Here he is with his wife, having a discussion with technicians.

Ever since Cuba was excluded from participation in the U.S. sugar market, other sugar-producing countries friendly to the U.S. have taken its place. These nations would inevitably be reluctant to part with their valuable share of the United States market.

RELATIONS WITH THE SOVIET UNION

Finally, there is the question of Cuba's new relationship with the Soviet Union and other countries of the Socialist bloc. These new friends have taken the place of the U.S. as Cuba's major trading partner, and source of technology and capital.

Most important of all, there is Cuba's economic dependency on the Soviet Union. Beginning in 1986, Cuba is obligated to make annual payments on its Soviet debt, which will stretch over a quarter of a century—until the year 2010. It is not likely that the Soviet Union will choose to ignore this debt, nor the influence in the New World it implies, any more than the U.S. has been willing to overlook the seizure by the Castro government of the assets of its citizens.

Pictures of Castro are ever-present, as here in the office of a judge in Cuba's Peoples Tribunal. By day the judge is a plumber!

In 1960 Fidel Castro met the late Soviet Premier, Nikita Khrushchev, at the United Nations General Assembly in New York.

Cane cutters carry stalks of sugar cane and machetes—the large knives used to cut the cane—as they march in a May Day parade.

4. THE PEOPLE

TODAY THERE are more than 8,600,000 people in Cuba. Cubans are lively, quick to laugh, ready with a barbed and often racy comment, and gifted in music and the arts. Cubans are talkative companions and good friends. They speak rapidly, and though Spanish is their language, Cuban Spanish is so rich in local sayings and idioms as to be almost a language of its own.

Official figures classify the Cuban population as 74 per cent white, 12 per cent black, and 14 per cent of mixed blood. But all such estimates of racial composition in Cuba are subject to substantial margins of error. Various races have so intermingled on the Caribbean island that it is impossible to classify the resulting population mixture with any accuracy.

Despite their Indian antecedents, the Cuban population has no full-blooded Indians. Even so, the imaginative visitor may detect here and there an "Indian-like" cast of features—a reminder that deep in the Cuban heritage there lingers some trace of Indian blood.

Those of Spanish descent comprise the dominant racial stock. Since the days of the Conquest, the ranks of the Spanish-descended have been periodically increased through immigration. Cuba has provided a safe asylum for refugees from the Spanish Civil War, and numerous exiles from other Latin American countries—driven by political upsets back home.

The racial composition of Cuba's ruling class was broadened somewhat, especially in the 19th

An allegorical dance at a folk festival tells of the days of slavery.

and 20th centuries, by immigrants from Europe, and the Far and Middle East. As elsewhere in the Caribbean, the Chinese, Lebanese and East Indians who have come to settle in Cuba, have shown less disposition to intermingle with races other than their own than have those of European stock.

The Spanish-descended still continue to hold most posts of importance in Cuba, while Cuban blacks have tended up to the present to remain at the bottom of the heap, economically, socially, and culturally. Few of the descendants of slaves have climbed the ladder of economic success, even under the Castro régime, which has repeatedly stressed racial equality.

While there is no readily apparent or officially approved prejudice in Cuba on racial matters, economic factors have tended to keep blacks in the lower job levels.

A dual standard also prevails in religion. The Castro government, in line with Marxist tenets, has chosen to downgrade the rôle of religion in everyday life, and the government itself has officially classified the country as "atheistic"—

The Catholic Church is still strong in Cuba—at Christmas, crèches are a familiar sight.

43

efforts by the revolutionary government to encourage people to stay on the land, there are indications that the urban proportion of the population is growing rapidly. To try to arrest this trend, the government has invested heavily in improving rural sectors of the national economy, and has de-emphasized investments even in Havana.

Cuba's population is heavily weighted at the age extremes, those either too old or too young to work. At present only about 35 per cent of the Cuban population figures in the nation's work-force, as contrasted with 42 per cent in the industrialized countries of Europe. This is of great concern to the government.

CULTURE

while maintaining diplomatic relations with the Vatican. But most Cubans today still remain devout and faithful Roman Catholics. They are baptized, married and buried under Church auspices. There is also a small number of Protestants, comprising about 3 or 4 per cent of the Cuban people.

The population is about evenly divided between the cities and the rural areas. Despite

As a city of great sophistication, Havana has generally tended to have something of an international feeling, and its musicians and painters were formerly as at home in New York or Paris as in their homeland. Artists from other lands have likewise found a congenial atmosphere in Havana. Among United States writers who called Cuba their second home, easily the most prominent was the late Ernest Hemingway. One

The School of Arts in Havana contains these unusual structures.

of the 20th century's best known novelists, he wrote movingly of the simple life of a Cuban fisherman in his famous work, *The Old Man and the Sea.*

During much of Cuban history, artistic works reflected intellectual currents elsewhere in the world—notably Europe, overlooking the rich vein of native folklore and the artistic, literary and musical potentialities of Cuban song and dance, all greatly indebted to African influences. It was as if Cubans lacked sufficient pride and self-confidence to value their own unique cultural heritage.

In *Cecilia Valdes*, however, one of the earliest of Cuban novels of real literary distinction, Cirilio Villaverde (1812–94) wrote the tragic story of a beautiful mulatto girl who was loved and betrayed by a Spanish-Cuban aristocrat. Villaverde's work set the stage for an appreciation of Cuba's own cultural values. This new appreciation gathered strength during the Cuban wars for independence, when a national spirit grew and was mobilized as an effective ally in the struggle.

The conga drummer beats out rhythms brought to Cuba by the African slaves.

One of the 20th century's well-known ballerinas, beautiful Alicia Alonso, was born in Cuba.

AFRO-CUBANISM

Early in the 20th century, Fernando Ortiz, the forerunner of the Afro-Cuban movement, wrote many influential works which brought widespread recognition to the merits of native Cuban themes. Ortiz and others contributed to the realization that black participation in the war against Spain had been decisive, and that black contributions to Cuban culture offered the greatest artistic potentialities.

By the 1920's, Cuban novelists, poets and musicians were strengthening national pride by presenting Afro-Cuban themes with great effect. Alejo Carpentier, in his novel *Ecue-Yamba-O*, dealt with Cuban voodoo, and made no secret of his conviction that Afro-Cubans are a superior, not a humble and inferior, breed. Poets —Nicolás Guillén, Ramón Guirao, José A. Tallet and Emilio Ballagas, as well as Carpentier —published powerfully rhythmic verse describing Cuban dancers writhing and contorting in the sensuality of African drum-beats. So influential did the Afro-Cubanists become that Ortiz could write with satisfaction that "in 1928 the drums began to beat in Cuban poetry."

Villaverde's novel as an operetta, *Cecilia Valdes*. He mixed many folkloric elements into his musical work, including such typical dances as the *guaracha, tango, conga, contradanza,* and *habañera*. Most of the music is Cuban, the Spanish musical themes being associated with the stage characters representing falseness and betrayal. "Afro" elements predominate in the music throughout, even appearing in the deeply moving finale, the *Sanctus*. Roig's work came precisely at the high point of the Afro-Cuban vogue, 1926–40, and gave respectability—in terms of the dominant culture of the outside world—to Afro-Cuban motifs. At the opening, an ex-slave tells how white lawyers robbed her of her money, a later lament bemoans the miserable life of the slave, and a lively *tango-conga* is sung in Afro-Cuban idioms that defy translation.

Afro-Cubanism evolved into an artistic movement of protest against racial discrimination, and it was also a vehicle for the expression of anti-Americanism. For example, Carpentier used the word, *sarambambiche* (the Cuban version of a well-known term of abuse) as a general name for Americans, whom he presented as incapable of understanding—much less sympathizing with—the complexities and magical subtleties of Afro-Cuban life.

MUSIC

In music, Ernesto Lecuona, during the 1920's and 1930's, was producing romantic and sensual Afro-Cuban music, which was as enthusiastically received and widely popular in the United States as in Cuba itself. His music, which included such compositions as *Malagueña* and *Siboney*, is still listened and danced to, and has become almost theme music identifying romantic Caribbean climes.

In 1932, Gonzalo Roig, founder of Havana's symphony orchestra and composer of many popular songs, presented his adaptation of

The School of Arts accommodates 675 boys and girls studying painting, music, acting, sculpture and ballet. These girls are having a lesson in African dancing.

The Teatro y Dansa Folklorique of Havana specializes in Afro-Cuban works derived from the traditions of the Yoruba tribes of Africa.

Afro-Cubanism seems to have declined as a literary and artistic movement by about 1940, although it never died completely, and during the Castro era it has even had a resurgence.

THE ARTS UNDER CASTRO

Cubans have made rich contributions to the world in thinkers and intellectuals—most widely admired of whom is doubtless José Martí. Like other Cuban men of thought, Martí was a leader

whose thoughts were wedded to action, and he died in the fight for independence.

Since the success of the Cuban Revolution in 1959, this characteristic has become the hallmark of the State, with government-approved decrees stating that the purpose of all of the arts should be to serve the nation. It is ironical that Martí's words are quoted both as supporting and opposing that idea.

Under Castro, artists from all fields must justify their production in terms of the Revolution, the interests of the people and nation. For this reason, Cuban architects, for example, have perforce become innovators in the construction of low-cost villages of conventional and prefabricated design and installation, as a contribution toward solving the nation's housing shortage. Cuban builders have become remarkably proficient in the use of standardized components in housing, again as an economical contribution to building cheap but sturdy housing. And they have pioneered in the construction of educational complexes—small cities really—designed for mass attendance at schools and universities.

All Cuban media—press, radio and television—likewise emphasize the accomplishment of revolutionary goals. Under the Castro

An old woman plays the rôle of a mourner during a folklore festival.

Carrying "farolas," the fanciful lanterns borne at Carnival time, these dancers bring a joyous atmosphere to July 26th, the anniversary of the Castro movement.

A member of the Cuban army performs in a ballet as his fellow soldiers watch with varying reactions. Ballet has attained new prominence in Cuba thanks to Soviet influence.

At Carnival time, before the beginning of Lent, Cubans dress in fanciful costumes and dance through the streets.

The National Festival of Farmers and Agricultural Workers is one of many worker festivals throughout the year.

The National School of Art at Marianao is under construction.

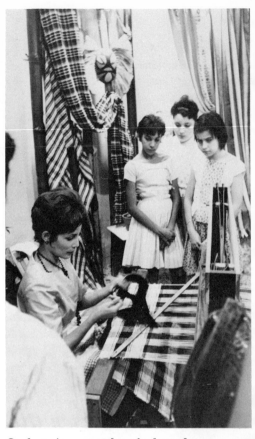

Pyrography—the art of burning designs into wood —is an art form receiving new attention in a government training school.

Students in arts and crafts learn how to weave on a hand loom.

régime, no criticism of the government is permitted, except for occasional and extremely forthright criticism uttered by Castro himself, and to some limited extent by lesser officials. All information is heavily saturated with propaganda, and written or produced to promote Marxist ideology.

Despite rigid control of all media, some Cuban works have found an admiring audience at home and abroad. One of these is poster art—

One of nine theatre groups operating in Havana, the Teatro Musical specializes in comedy (called "bufo" in Cuba). Members of the troupe are seen in "Pato Macho," a musical comedy satirizing "machismo," or male chauvinism.

The Cuban state strongly encourages arts and crafts, such as the metal work this man is doing.

A wood-carver puts the finishing touches on a statuette of a deer.

posters have become under Castro a prime vehicle for communicating with the masses and artists of considerable talent have been attracted to poster production.

Another is Cuban cinema—on modest budgets, Cuban film-makers have produced excellent short films, many of them remarkably candid and moving documentaries on social and political themes. These productions are virtually unknown to audiences in the United States, where distributors have been reluctant to make them available. However, they have won theatre festival prizes elsewhere in the world, in competitions, for example, in Moscow, Leipzig, and London.

A poster in French announces the First Tricontinental Congress, a meeting in Havana in 1966 of delegates from the "have-not" nations of Asia, Africa and Latin America.

Cuban youngsters, like their counterparts elsewhere, enjoy the spun-sugar sweetness of cotton candy.

FOOD

Despite the pervasive influence of the Revolution, the old eating customs still prevail in Cuba, whenever there is a supply of the ingredients. *Picadillo*, ground meat served in a sauce, usually with rice, is a common dish. Others are *moros y cristianos*—Moors and Christians—a tasty combination of white rice and black beans, and *ropa vieja*—old clothes—a concoction of shredded meat, rice and almost anything else handy, which, while it may look unappealing, is good to eat. On Christmas Eve, the traditional main dish is roast suckling pig. For dessert, cream cheese with *guava* preserve, a fruit jelly, is often served. After dinner, Cuban men are likely to smoke cigars, the finest of which have traditionally come from Cuba's westernmost province, Pinar del Rio.

Cuba has a great variety of seafood, including red snapper, kingfish, and swordfish. There are also lobster-like ocean crayfish, the large Moro crab, a famous delicacy, and the much esteemed small oysters from Sagua la Grande. A popular dish is *paella*, rice with as great a variety of fish and shellfish as can be had—including squid, octopus, crab, oysters, crayfish, clams, and mussels, if possible.

The Cuban national basketball team beat the United States (white uniforms) in the Central American Games held in Quito, Ecuador, in 1971.

Fidel Castro is well known for his habit of showing up unannounced. Here he happened to be passing some schoolboys playing basketball and stopped to join in the game.

SPORTS

Cubans are very keen on sports, and the Castro government has promoted sports participation as a matter of national policy. Cuban athletes play all the games familiar to people in other countries—football (soccer), and tennis, for example—and are likely to play them very well. Sports which originated in the United States are very popular—especially baseball, softball and basketball. Many Cubans have become star players on big-league U.S. baseball teams. During the season, there is scarcely an open space in Havana without a baseball game in progress, played by either men or boys.

Volleyball is a popular sport among the youth of Cuba.

53

Chess has long been a popular game in Cuba, where chess tournaments attract leading players from all over the world.

Cubans have also achieved international distinction in boxing, basketball, rowing, sailing, swimming—and some years ago a Cuban won the world's championship in chess.

FAMILY LIFE

Cuban family relationships have customarily been strong and extensive. Families are closely knit, with meaningful relationships that include second, third, fourth, and even more distant cousins. The so-called "extended family" is an important institution, with families taking care of their own during hard times. Another important relationship in Cuba is that of the "padrino," or godfather, who really is expected to exercise responsibility with respect to the rearing and education of his godchild.

Women, traditionally sheltered in Cuban society, have emerged to work side by side with men, in a wide range of activities.

HEALTH, EDUCATION AND WELFARE

In pursuing the goals of the Cuban Revolution, the Castro régime has enormously increased the proportion of government spending for social progress—better health, education

Gymnasts form a striking tableau during a Cuban sports festival.

Modern day-care facilities are now available for the children of working mothers.

It is washday and these young women have found a shady spot to wring out the clothes.

An estimated 100,000 Cuban school children are now engaged in teaching their illiterate elders to read and write.

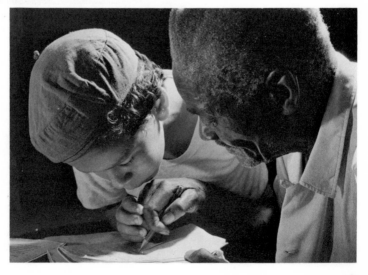

Botany students on a field trip study plant classification on the spot.

and welfare. Before Castro came to power, only 8,000 Cubans worked in public health, but a decade later, there were nearly 90,000. Before Castro, Cuba's school enrolment was less than 1,000,000 young people, but a decade later, the figure stood at 2,200,000.

Cuban government spending for social security, health and education quadrupled over the first 10 years of the Revolution. The government now provides nearly 300,000 scholarships for students, as against less than 16,000 before Castro.

Camp Columbia, near Havana, once a military headquarters, is now used for educational activities.

This interesting building is the home of the National Centre of Scientific Research.

From this huge storage shed at the port of Cienfuegos, granulated raw sugar is carried by conveyor belt to ships moored in the port.

5. THE ECONOMY

THE ZAFRA, or sugar harvest, is the most crucial event in the annual life of the Cuban economy, because sugar alone represents nearly 80 per cent of the island's total earnings overseas. The harvesting is a backbreaking operation, one requiring dawn-to-dark work in the sugar fields by men, women—even children.

In spite of advances in the manufacture of farm machinery, there is not yet a satisfactory method for harvesting the tall, tough stalks of Cuban cane by machine. It must all be done by hand. With two blows from the *machete*, a long sharp knife, the harvester slashes off the long leaves. A third slash of the *machete* is required to sever the stalk from its roots, as close as possible to the ground.

The cane cutters move slowly, methodically through the fields—in long formations—before them endless stands of tall cane, waving with the breeze, behind them felled cane stalks which must be loaded aboard flat trucks and taken to the sugar mill. At the mills the sugar cane undergoes several processes in its conversion into sugar and such other sugar by-products as molasses and rum. The harvest season lasts from early December to May, and even longer, weather conditions permitting. The slashing of the machete in the fields is a symbol of Cuba and its main problem.

ONE-CROP ECONOMY

Throughout much of its history Cuba has been tyrannized by its dependency on sugar. During centuries of Spanish rule, sugar cane production was built into the fabric of Cuban life. Large numbers of unskilled workers and

Inside the storage shed, a bulldozer pushes the sugar into piles.

Raw sugar cane, ready to be processed, is fed into a mill that has been modernized with Soviet aid.

Cuban workers meet members of the Venceremos Brigade, a group of United States volunteers who have helped harvest the sugar cane, among other things.

In the old days, ox carts were used to haul sugar cane to the mill, after the stalks were cut and stripped in the fields.

In Cuba, everyone who can be spared works in the fields during the sugar harvest, even children as young as this one.

large tracts of land were required for the operation of a profitable sugar cane estate. Like other areas of the world, where the economy depends on such plantation-produced crops as sugar and cotton, Cuban society was divided at an early date into masters and slaves.

The Spanish overlord enjoyed a big and luxurious home, vacations abroad, and a fine education for his children. The blacks who were imported in bondage to cut the cane, led a life of deprivation, with miserable working and living conditions on the masters' estate.

A brief break in this serfdom was provided by the U.S. military authorities, who placed Cuba under martial law after the Spanish-American War. These soldier-rulers abolished the plantation system, and the way was cleared for increased ownership of the sugar lands and mills by local Cuban interests. During this transitional period, there emerged in Cuba thousands of independent tenant farmers, proud owners of small plots of land.

Unhappily, the vicious economic cycle started over again, as large corporations moved into the vacuum created by the departure of the Spanish

masters. The tenant farmers were at the mercy of the large sugar cane mills—the men or corporations with the mills and the largest tracts of land—who in turn were at the mercy of the prices paid for sugar in world commerce. For Cuba, this reliance on world prices for sugar, over which Cuba has little or no control, has meant periods of "boom" or "bust," as the prices have risen sharply or dropped suddenly.

At the end of World War I, for example, sugar was in great demand and sold for 22.5 cents per pound. But within six months of the peak, it had dropped to less than four cents. Four years later, the price was one-half cent per pound.

As the economic depression of the Cuban sugar industry deepened, tenant farmers, forced into bankruptcy, were obliged to sell off their lands for next to nothing, before sinking into complete poverty. Smaller mills and corporations were likewise forced to sell off their sugar assets to the larger corporations, which alone had resources enough to wait out the depression in sugar prices.

Many of these corporations were owned by

In Cuba no one has the right to be idle—one must be either working, in the army or in school. These girls, aged 16 to 22, are part of the Columna Juvenil del Centenario, a work brigade assigned to develop the province of Camaguey.

United States interests. By the late 1920's, 70 per cent of the "Cuban" sugar industry was U.S.-owned. And there was resentment among the mass of the Cuban people. This basic anger against foreign ownership had helped fuel the Cuban independence movement, and would in time work for Fidel Castro's revolution—even though the U.S. share of the Cuban sugar industry had dropped to less than 40 per cent in the year before Castro came into power.

GOVERNMENT OWNERSHIP

Though the nation's sugar industry is government-owned today, there is still resentment over the prices paid by the nation, and by new-found socialist allies. For the fact remains that Cuba is still chained to sugar, of which the U.S. buys none.

If there has been a change under Castro, it is mainly in the success with which he has ex-

Sacks of processed sugar are loaded aboard a cargo ship for export.

Young coffee trees are sprayed in order to kill insect pests. Coffee formerly was grown only in the mountains of Cuba, but today it is planted widely in the lowlands, especially those near Havana.

Women now work side by side with men in Cuban factories.

horted Cuban people, those from all walks of life, to take a hand in the sugar harvest. His success has been all the more remarkable, in that in making his countrymen realize their utter dependency on sugar he has at the same time built a sense of Cuban unity around the sugar issue. But beneath the surface there simmers resentment at Cuba's socialist-bloc friends. At issue, as Castro himself has repeatedly stressed, is the problem that increases in Cuban sugar prices are not enough to offset the increases Cuba must pay to import necessary products and machines.

ECONOMIC DIVERSIFICATION

Since the Castro government came to power, it has made intense efforts to diversify the range of products made in Cuba. The result is that Cuba today produces cement and steel bars, fertilizers and farm machinery, rayon and other fabrics, tires and batteries, paper and cardboard, shoes and bottles, soap and toothpaste—and a number of other products not produced in sufficient quantities prior to the Revolution.

61

Humped Brahma cattle are resistant to ticks, the blood-sucking pests that can cause serious damage, even death, to cattle. For this reason, the Cuban government is promoting Brahmas as part of its campaign to improve beef production.

The Castro régime has also quadrupled the nation's catch of fish, with Soviet technical assistance, and has invested heavily in increasing beef production, to breed more valuable cattle and to enrich the pasture lands grazed by some 5,000,000 head of livestock.

With one of the highest per capita incomes in Latin America, Cuba under Castro has succeeded in making the island less dependent than ever before on imported products. Visitors to the island report that psychologically this drive has had a deep impact on the Cuban people. The nationalization of all important industry in Cuba has resulted in Cuban pride in Cuban ownership of all of the sources and profits of wealth.

But Cuba still relies on many imported products for survival—including such basic foods as rice, wheat, flour, lard, vegetable oils, dried beans and peas, and salted fish. Other necessary items, buses and trucks and spare parts, for example, must likewise be imported—as well as petroleum, without which the Cuban economy would come to a halt.

As desirable as the benefits of a totally managed economy may seem, they cost money, as does the maintenance of more than 1,000,000 Cubans in the nation's defense establishment—a figure including part-time militiamen.

Cuba would not have been able to avoid bankruptcy had it not been able to draw on the Soviet Union. Cuba has had to depend on the

Pineapples are now grown in Cuba with the aid of modern agricultural machines, such as this tractor.

Shipbuilders are busy constructing a fishing boat in a Cuban shipyard.

Russians for imports of more than 5,000,000 tons of fuel annually. Without this energy, as Castro himself has declared, Cuba would not have the power to brighten its lights, turn its lathes, and run its engines. For Cuba has little coal, and virtually no hydro-electric power potential. The obvious conclusion is that without Soviet aid, estimated to total about U.S. $2,000,000 a day—and representing 55 per cent of all the Soviet Union's foreign aid—the Cuban economy would collapse.

Castro himself has frequently acknowledged the indebtedness of the Cuban economy to the help of the Soviets. Castro has likewise openly criticized his own régime for its bureaucratic failings—poor management that has led to pile-ups of supplies, slowdowns in the nation's factories, and production short-falls.

Whatever the judgment of history on the Cuban economy under Castro, there remains the fact of its dependency on Soviet assistance. There remains also the truth that the economy is managed in all its aspects by a single man, a remarkable man who runs Cuba with wide-spread popular support, and with energy and dynamism. Whether any man should have such powers, no matter how brilliant he may be, is the question that history must answer over the long term.

A young woman learns to handle a lathe at a Soviet-equipped vocational school.

INDEX

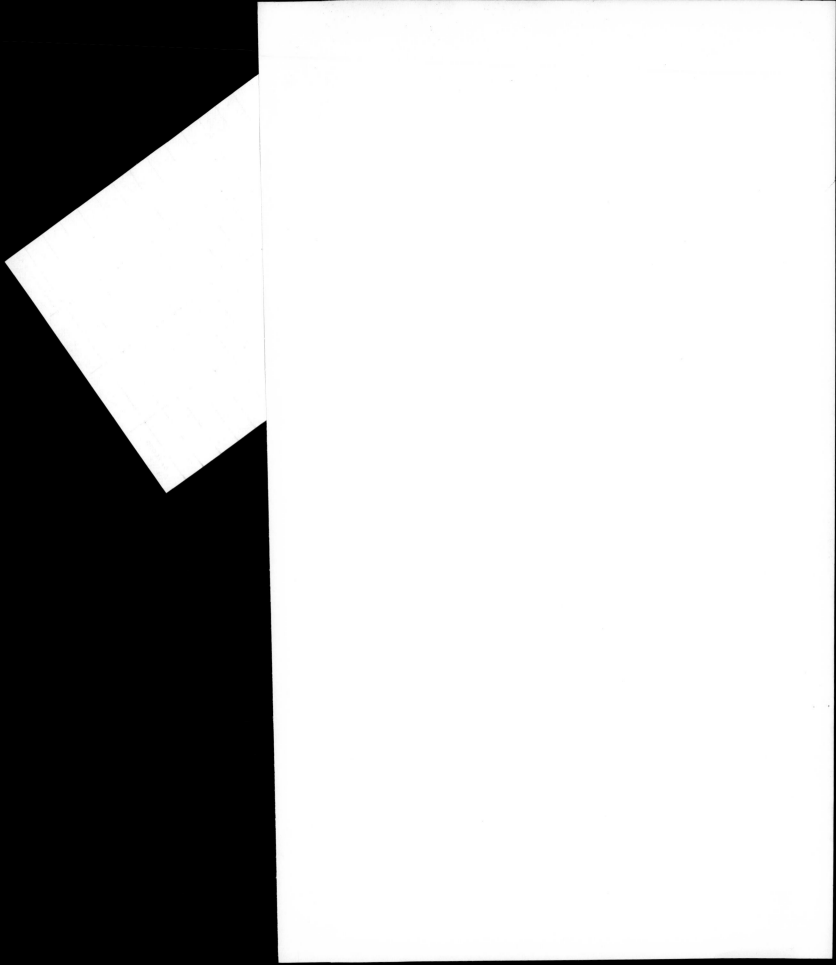

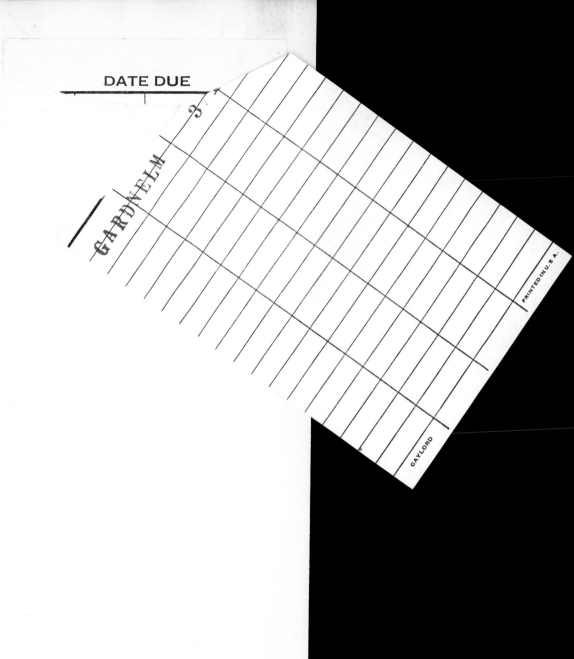